WAFFLES

EXCITING NEW WAYS TO USE YOUR WAFFLE MAKER!

D1317108

pil

Publications International, Ltd.

Pictured on the front cover: Chocolate Chip Ice Cream Sandwiches (*page 103*).

Pictured on the back cover *(left to right):* Garlic Bread Waffle Sticks *(page 78)*, Waffled Burger Sliders *(page 66)*, Monkey Waffle Bites *(page 65)*, Belgian Leige Waffles *(page 7)*, Cheesy Mashed Potato Waffles *(page 87)*, Crab Cake Waffles with Garlic Dipping Sauce *(page 42)*, BLT Waffle-Wiches *(page 88)*, and Waffled French Toast *(page 80)*.

ISBN: 978-1-68022-698-0

Library of Congress Control Number: 2016947355

Manufactured in China.

8 7 6 5 4 3 2 1

Microwave Cooking: Microwave ovens vary in wattage. Use the cooking times as guidelines and check for doneness before adding more time.

Preparation/Cooking Times: Preparation times are based on the approximate amount of time required to assemble the recipe before cooking, baking, chilling or serving. These times include preparation steps such as measuring, chopping and mixing. The fact that some preparations and cooking can be done simultaneously is taken into account. Preparation of optional ingredients and serving suggestions is not included.

TABLE OF CONTENTS

CHOOSING A WAFFLE MAKER

Waffle makers are no longer just used for breakfast. There are so many recipes available for everything from classic ideas, snacks, dinners, and even desserts. Before you get started, decide what features are most important for you and your family.

STYLE?

Primarily, you'll end up choosing between a Belgian waffle maker (one that has deeper pockets with big craters that tends to make a large fluffier waffle and a traditional, standard waffle maker that has shallow compartments and cooks up a crispier waffle. Professional-grade, flip-over models are also available for home use. There are stove-top waffle makers available, too.

Belgian Waffles

Standard Waffles

SIZE AND SHAPE?

Depending on the size of your family or how many waffles you want to make at a time, you can choose between a larger or smaller waffle maker. Plus, you can choose varying shapes including round, square, mini, heart- or animal-shaped, for example.

TYPE OF SURFACE?

Today, most makers offer a nonstick surface to help with easier cleanup, but some offer dishwasher-safe removable plates, others overflow batter catchers, and still others offer interchangeable plates to make sandwiches and paninis.

TYPE OF INDICATORS?

Higher-end waffle makers may feature lights that notify you when waffles are done or adjustable thermostats to help decide between a fluffy or crispy waffle. Others include a dial or an indicator slide for preferences on browning and crispiness.

STORAGE?

Tuck-away cords and feet for standup storage may also be important to you when space is limited.

Whatever shape or type of waffle maker you choose, you'll enjoy experimenting with it. Choose any number of great recipe ideas inside.

WAFFLE HACKS

Waffle makers aren't just for waffles anymore. You'll be surprised at how many different fun and creative foods you can make. Try some of our favorite waffle "hacks:"

BANANA BREAD WAFFLES:

Refrigerate a loaf of banana bread. Slice it into ½ to ¾-inch slices; place in heated waffle maker. Cook about 2 minutes* until browned and crispy. Drizzle with maple syrup, if desired.

PIZZA CRUST:

Roll out store-bought refrigerated pizza dough to fit waffle maker. Cook for 2 to 4 minutes* or until browned and crisp. Remove dough and top with marinara sauce and cheese. Heat under broiler 1 to 2 minutes until cheese is melted.

CHOCOLATE CHIP COOKIES:

Start with refrigerated cookie dough; cut into bite-sized pieces and place in heated waffle maker. Cook 3 to 5 minutes* until cookies are browned and crispy.

CINNAMON ROLLS:

Start with refrigerated cinnamon roll dough; separate rolls and place in heated waffle maker. Cook 3 to 5 minutes* until browned and crispy. Drizzle with cream cheese frosting.

BROWNIES:

Start with refrigerated brownie dough; cut into bite-sized pieces and place in heated waffle maker. Cook 3 to 5 minutes* until brownies are browned and crispy. Sprinkle with powdered sugar, if desired.

TATER TOTS WAFFLES:

Start with frozen tater tots. Place side-by-side in heated waffle maker. Cook 4 to 6 minutes* or until browned and crispy. Top with salt, black pepper, hot pepper sauce or ketchup, if desired.

NOTE: Be sure to spray waffle maker with nonstick cooking spray before heating.

Some waffle makers cook quicker than others. Check waffle maker's manufacturer's directions for most accurate cooking times.

CLASSIC FAVORITES

BELGIAN LEIGE WAFFLES

MAKES 12 WAFFLES

½ teaspoon granulated sugar

2 teaspoons active dry yeast

½ cup warm milk

1½ cups all-purpose flour

1 teaspoon ground cinnamon

2 teaspoons vanilla

½ teaspoon salt

2 eggs

½ cup unsalted butter, softened, cut into small pieces

½ cup pearl sugar, turbindo sugar or crushed sugar cubes

1. Dissolve granulated sugar and yeast in warm milk in large bowl of electric mixer. Cover 5 minutes or until bubbly. Add flour, cinnamon, vanilla, salt and eggs to mixer bowl. Beat with dough hook until fully combined and stiff. Cover with damp towel; set aside in warm place 30 minutes.

2. Beat in butter, one piece at a time, with dough hook until butter is incorporated and dough is smooth and elastic. Remove to work surface; knead in sugar crystals.

3. Divide dough into 12 balls; place on plate. Cover; set aside in warm place 30 minutes.

4. Preheat waffle maker to medium. Place dough ball onto waffle maker; cook about 2 to 3 minutes or until golden brown and crisp. Remove to plate*.

*Use caution when removing waffles from waffle maker. The sugar cubes can be extremely hot.

SUNNY SEED BRAN WAFFLES

MAKES 4 WAFFLES

2 egg whites

1 tablespoon packed dark brown sugar

1 tablespoon canola or vegetable oil

1 cup fat-free (skim) milk

⅔ cup unprocessed wheat bran

⅔ cup quick oats

1½ teaspoons baking powder

¼ teaspoon salt

3 tablespoons sunflower seeds, toasted*

1 cup apple butter

*To toast sunflower seeds, cook and stir in small nonstick skillet over medium heat about 5 minutes or until golden brown. Remove from skillet; let cool.

1. Beat egg whites in medium bowl with electric mixer until soft peaks form. Blend brown sugar and oil in small bowl. Stir in milk; mix well.

2. Combine bran, oats, baking powder and salt in large bowl; mix well. Stir milk mixture into bran mixture. Add sunflower seeds; stir just until moistened. *Do not overmix.* Gently fold in beaten egg whites.

3. Spray nonstick waffle maker lightly with nonstick cooking spray; heat according to manufacturer's directions. Stir batter; spoon ½ cup batter into waffle maker for each waffle. Cook until steam stops escaping from around edges and waffle is golden brown. Serve each waffle with ¼ cup apple butter.

NOTE: It is essential to use a nonstick waffle maker because of the low fat content of these waffles.

WAFFLES

MAKES ABOUT 6 ROUND WAFFLES

2¼ cups all-purpose
   flour

2 tablespoons sugar

1 tablespoon
   baking powder

½ teaspoon salt

2 cups milk

2 eggs, beaten

¼ cup vegetable oil

1. Preheat waffle maker; grease lightly.

2. Sift flour, sugar, baking powder and salt in large bowl. Combine milk, eggs and oil in medium bowl. Stir liquid ingredients into dry ingredients until moistened.

3. For each waffle, pour about ¾ cup batter onto waffle maker. Close lid and bake until steaming stops. Garnish as desired.

CHOCOLATE WAFFLES: Substitute ¼ cup unsweetened cocoa powder for ¼ cup flour and add ¼ teaspoon vanilla extract to liquid ingredients. Proceed as directed above.

TIP: For crispier waffles, use less batter and let them cook for a few seconds longer after the steaming has stopped.

GLUTEN-FREE WAFFLES

MAKES 5 (6-INCH) WAFFLES

2 **eggs**

½ **cup plain low-fat yogurt**

½ **cup whole milk**

1 **cup Gluten-Free All-Purpose Flour Blend (recipe follows)***

1 **tablespoon sugar**

1 **teaspoon baking powder**

1 **teaspoon baking soda**

½ **teaspoon salt**

2 **tablespoons butter, melted**

Maple syrup and additional butter

Or use any all-purpose gluten-free flour blend that does not contain xanthan gum.

1. Preheat waffle maker according to manufacturer's directions.

2. Beat eggs in large bowl until light and fluffy. Whisk in yogurt and milk.

3. Combine flour blend, sugar, baking powder, baking soda and salt in medium bowl. Gradually whisk yogurt mixture into flour mixture until smooth. Whisk in 2 tablespoons butter.

4. Add batter to waffle maker by ½ cupfuls for 6-inch waffles (or adjust amount depending on waffle maker). Bake until crisp and browned. Serve with maple syrup and additional butter.

NOTE: Refrigerate or freeze leftover waffles; reheat in toaster oven until crisp.

GLUTEN-FREE ALL-PURPOSE FLOUR BLEND

MAKES ABOUT 5 CUPS

1 **cup white rice flour**

1 **cup sorghum flour**

1 **cup tapioca flour**

1 **cup cornstarch**

1 **cup almond flour or coconut flour**

Combine all ingredients in large bowl. Whisk to make sure flours are evenly distributed. The recipe can be doubled or tripled. Store in airtight container in the refrigerator.

LEMON POPPY SEED WAFFLES WITH FRESH BLUEBERRIES

MAKES 6 SERVINGS

1½ cups fresh or frozen blueberries, thawed

½ cup plus 1 teaspoon sugar substitute,* divided

¾ cup all-purpose flour

⅓ cup whole wheat flour

2 teaspoons poppy seeds

½ teaspoon baking powder

¼ teaspoon baking soda

⅛ teaspoon salt

½ cup buttermilk

¾ cup cholesterol-free egg substitute

1 tablespoon canola oil

1 teaspoon grated lemon peel

½ teaspoon vanilla

1 teaspoon powdered sugar

This recipe was tested with sucralose-based sugar substitute.

1. Combine blueberries and 1 teaspoon sugar substitute in small microwavable bowl. Microwave on MEDIUM (50%) 3 to 4 minutes or until warm. Set aside.

2. Combine flours, remaining ½ cup sugar substitute, poppy seeds, baking powder, baking soda, and salt in medium bowl; stir to mix well.

3. Combine buttermilk, egg substitute, oil, lemon peel and vanilla in another medium bowl; stir to combine. Add buttermilk mixture to flour mixture; stir just until moistened.

4. Spray waffle maker with nonstick cooking spray; preheat. Spoon about ¼ cup batter into waffle maker, spreading batter to edges. Cook 4 to 5 minutes or until steaming stops. Repeat with remaining batter.

5. Sprinkle waffles with powdered sugar. Serve with blueberry sauce.

EASY WAFFLES

MAKES 3 (9-INCH) WAFFLES

1⅔ cups all-purpose flour

⅓ cup nonfat dry milk

3 tablespoons sugar

1½ teaspoons baking powder

1½ teaspoons baking soda

1½ teaspoons salt

½ teaspoon ground cinnamon

⅛ teaspoon ground nutmeg

1¼ cups (10 ounces) sparkling or still water

2 tablespoons corn or vegetable oil

1 egg

¼ teaspoon orange extract

1. Preheat and prepare waffle maker according to manufacturer's instructions.

2. Combine flour, milk, sugar, baking powder, baking soda, salt, cinnamon and nutmeg in medium bowl. Stir in water, oil, egg and orange extract with wire whisk or fork until most lumps are gone. Let rest 5 minutes.

3. Pour heaping ¾-cup mixture onto prepared waffle maker. Cook until steaming stops. Repeat with remaining batter. Serve immediately.

BUTTERMILK PECAN WAFFLES

MAKES 6 WAFFLES

PREP TIME: 5 minutes **START TO FINISH TIME:** 15 minutes

- 2 cups all-purpose flour
- ⅓ cup CREAM OF WHEAT® Hot Cereal (Instant, 1-minute, 2½-minute or 10-minute cook time), uncooked
- 4 teaspoons baking powder
- 1 cup milk
- 1 cup buttermilk
- 2 eggs
- 6 tablespoons butter, melted
- 1 cup chopped pecans

1. Combine flour, Cream of Wheat and baking powder in medium bowl; set aside.

2. Beat milk, buttermilk and eggs in mixing bowl with wire whisk until well blended. Stir Cream of Wheat mixture into egg mixture. Add melted butter and mix well to combine. Stir in pecans.

3. Pour into hot waffle iron and bake until golden brown.

TIP: Top the waffles with fresh fruit and whipped cream for a decadent breakfast or dessert.

OATMEAL WAFFLES WITH SPICED APPLE COMPOTE

MAKES 6 SERVINGS

COMPOTE

- **2 tablespoons unsalted butter**
- **1 pound Granny Smith apples, peeled, cored and cut into ½-inch pieces**
- **¼ cup maple syrup**
- **½ cup water**
- **¼ cup raisins**
- **1 teaspoon ground cinnamon**

WAFFLES

- **1¼ cups quick-cooking oats**
- **¾ cup oat flour**
- **¼ cup flax meal**
- **½ teaspoon salt**
- **1 tablespoon baking powder**
- **1¾ cups hot milk**
- **8 tablespoons (1 stick) unsalted butter, melted and slightly cooled**
- **3 eggs**
- **¼ cup maple syrup**

1. Preheat Belgium waffle maker to medium-high heat. Set wire rack on top of large baking sheet; place in oven.

2. Prepare compote. Melt 2 table-spoons butter in large nonstick skillet over medium-high heat. Add apples, ¼ cup syrup, water, raisins and cinnamon; stir to combine. Reduce heat to medium, cover and cook 5 minutes. Uncover; continue cooking 5 minutes or until apples are tender and most of liquid has evaporated, stirring occasionally. Set aside.

3. Prepare waffles. Combine oats, flour, flax meal, salt and baking powder in large bowl. Pour in hot milk; stir until combined. Let stand 5 minutes.

4. Combine 8 tablespoons melted butter, eggs and ¼ cup syrup in large bowl. Pour into oat mixture; stir until combined.

5. Pour ⅓ cup batter into each well of waffle maker. Close lid; cook 6 minutes or until golden brown. Remove waffles to wire rack in oven; keep warm. Repeat with remaining batter.

6. Serve waffles with apple compote.

FESTIVE CRANBERRY WAFFLES

MAKES 4 (7-INCH) ROUND WAFFLES

1 cup all-purpose flour

½ cup dried cranberries coarsely chopped

⅓ cup sugar

⅓ cup yellow cornmeal

2 teaspoons baking powder

1 teaspoon orange peel

½ teaspoon baking soda

½ teaspoon ground cinnamon

¼ teaspoon salt

1 cup buttermilk*

¼ cup plus ½ cup milk or orange juice, divided

1 egg

1 teaspoon vanilla

3 tablespoons butter, melted

Toppings: butter, maple syrup and powdered sugar (optional)

*If you don't have buttermilk, substitute ½ cup milk or orange juice and ¾ cup plain yogurt. Add a small amount of additional milk if batter is too thick.

1. Preheat waffle maker.

2. Combine flour, dried cranberries, sugar, cornmeal, baking powder, orange peel, baking soda, cinnamon and salt in large bowl; stir until well blended. Whisk buttermilk, ¼ cup milk, egg and vanilla in medium bowl; add to flour mixture, stirring just until moistened. Stir in melted butter. Add additional milk, 1 tablespoon at a time, if batter is too thick.

3. Spray waffle maker with nonstick cooking spray. Spoon about ¾ cup batter onto waffle maker. Close lid; bake until steaming stops or waffles are brown and crispy. Serve immediately with desired toppings.

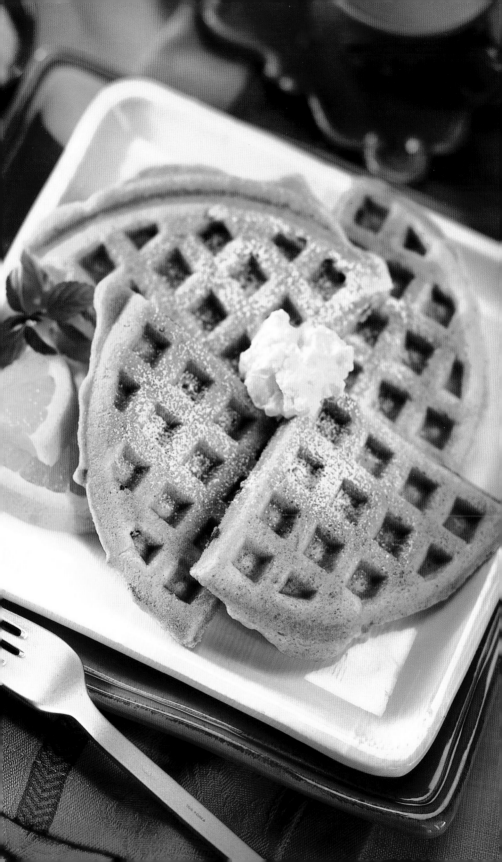

CHOCOLATE WAFFLES

MAKES ABOUT 6 WAFFLES

2 cups all-purpose
  flour

¼ cup unsweetened
  cocoa powder

2 tablespoons sugar

1 tablespoon
  baking powder

½ teaspoon salt

2 cups milk

2 eggs, beaten

¼ cup vegetable oil

1 teaspoon vanilla

  Raspberry Syrup
  (recipe follows)

1. Preheat waffle maker; grease lightly.

2. Sift flour, cocoa, sugar, baking powder and salt into large bowl. Combine milk, eggs, oil and vanilla in small bowl. Stir liquid ingredients into dry ingredients until moistened.

3. For each waffle, pour about ¾ cup batter into waffle maker. Close lid and bake until steaming stops. Serve with Raspberry Syrup.

RASPBERRY SYRUP

MAKES ABOUT 1⅓ CUPS

1 cup water

1 cup sugar

1 package
  (10 ounces)
  frozen
  raspberries in
  syrup

1. Combine water and sugar in large saucepan. Cook over medium heat, stirring constantly, until sugar has dissolved. Continue cooking until mixture thickens slightly, about 10 minutes.

2. Stir in frozen raspberries; cook, stirring, until berries are thawed. Bring to a boil; continue cooking 5 to 10 minutes or until syrup thickens slightly. Serve warm.

BANANA-NUT BUTTERMILK WAFFLES

MAKES 4 SERVINGS

¾ cup walnuts or pecans, plus additional for garnish

2 cups all-purpose flour

¼ cup sugar

2 teaspoons baking powder

1 teaspoon salt

2 eggs, separated

2 cups buttermilk

2 very ripe bananas, mashed (about 1 cup)

¼ cup (½ stick) butter, melted

1 teaspoon vanilla

Maple syrup and banana slices

1. Toast walnuts in medium nonstick skillet over medium heat 5 minutes or until fragrant, stirring frequently. Transfer to plate to cool; chop and set aside.

2. Lightly coat waffle maker with nonstick cooking spray; preheat according to manufacturer's directions.

3. Meanwhile, combine flour, sugar, baking powder and salt in large bowl. Beat egg yolks in medium bowl. Add buttermilk, mashed bananas, butter, vanilla and ¾ cup walnuts; mix well. Stir buttermilk mixture into flour mixture just until moistened.

4. Beat egg whites in medium bowl with electric mixer at high speed until stiff but not dry. Fold egg whites into batter.

5. Pour ¾ cup batter into waffle maker; cook 4 to 6 minutes or until golden. Repeat with remaining batter. Serve with maple syrup and banana slices. Garnish with additional walnuts.

TROPICAL ORANGE WAFFLES

MAKES 4 SERVINGS

PREP AND COOK TIME: 30 minutes

WAFFLES

- **2 tablespoons macadamia nuts**
- **1 cup all-purpose flour**
- **½ cup whole-wheat flour**
- **1 tablespoon sugar**
- **1½ teaspoons baking powder**
- **¼ teaspoon salt**
- **1 cup Florida orange juice**
- **1 egg**
- **1 tablespoon canola oil**
- **1 teaspoon pure vanilla extract**

BANANA COCONUT SYRUP

- **½ cup Florida orange juice**
- **2 tablespoons coconut milk**
- **¼ cup maple syrup**
- **1 banana, sliced**

1. Toast nuts in 350°F degree oven 5 to 8 minutes until golden. Cool and chop; set aside.

2. In large bowl, combine flours, sugar, baking powder and salt. In medium bowl, combine orange juice, egg, canola oil and vanilla and mix well. Add liquid ingredients to dry ingredients and mix until smooth; stir in nuts.

3. For syrup, simmer orange juice in saucepan over low heat to reduce by half. Add coconut milk, maple syrup and sliced banana to warm through.

4. Heat waffle iron and lightly coat with nonstick canola oil spray. Pour ½ cup batter on warmed waffle iron. Cook until golden brown or until waffle begins to separate from iron.

5. Top waffle with ¼ cup banana coconut syrup. Serve immediately.

Courtesy of Florida Department of Citrus

PEACH AND SAUSAGE WAFFLES

MAKES 6 SERVINGS

- ½ **pound BOB EVANS® Original Recipe Roll Sausage**
- 1 **cup all-purpose flour**
- 3 **tablespoons sugar**
- 2 **teaspoons baking powder**
- 2 **eggs**
- 2 **cups milk**
- 4 **tablespoons melted butter**
- 1 **cup chopped, drained canned peaches**

Preheat waffle iron. If preparing waffles in advance, preheat oven to 200°F. Crumble and cook sausage in medium skillet until browned; drain on paper towels. Whisk flour, sugar and baking powder in large bowl. Whisk eggs and milk in medium bowl until well blended. Pour liquid ingredients over dry ingredients; whisk until just combined. Stir in butter until blended. Stir in peaches and sausage. Lightly butter grids of waffle iron; add ½ cup batter to hot iron. Cook waffles according to manufacturer's instructions. Serve immediately or hold in oven until ready to serve.

CORNMEAL WAFFLES

MAKES 9 TO 10 WAFFLES

1¾ cups yellow
   cake mix with
   pudding in the
   mix*

½ cup all-purpose
   flour

½ cup cornmeal

1 teaspoon baking
   powder

2 cups whole milk

6 tablespoons
   unsalted butter,
   melted

2 eggs

   Additional butter
   (optional)

   Maple syrup
   (optional)

Save remainder for future use.

1. Preheat oven to 200°F. Place wire rack on top of baking sheet; place in oven. Preheat waffle maker according to manufacturer's directions. Coat cooking surface with nonstick cooking spray.

2. Combine cake mix, flour, cornmeal and baking powder in large bowl; mix well. Combine milk, melted butter and eggs in medium bowl; mix well. Add to dry ingredients; mix until no lumps remain.

3. Pour ½ cup batter into waffle maker. Cook until steaming stops and waffle is golden brown and crisp. Transfer to wire rack on baking sheet in oven to keep warm. Repeat with remaining batter. Serve with butter and maple syrup, if desired.

VANILLA MULTIGRAIN WAFFLES

MAKES 4 WAFFLES

1 cup low-fat buttermilk

¼ cup steel cut oats

⅓ cup all-purpose flour

⅓ cup whole wheat flour

1 teaspoon baking powder

½ teaspoon baking soda

¼ teaspoon salt

1 egg

2 tablespoons packed brown sugar

1 tablespoon vegetable oil

1 teaspoon vanilla

Maple syrup (optional)

1. Combine buttermilk and oats in large bowl; let stand 10 minutes. Spray waffle maker with nonstick cooking spray; preheat according to manufacturer's directions.

2. Combine all-purpose flour, whole wheat flour, baking powder, baking soda and salt in medium bowl; mix well.

3. Whisk egg, brown sugar, oil and vanilla in small bowl until smooth and well blended. Stir into oat mixture. Add flour mixture; stir until smooth and well blended.

4. Pour ⅔ cup batter into waffle maker; cook about 5 minutes until steaming stops and waffle is golden brown. Repeat with remaining batter. Serve with syrup, if desired.

BEIGNET WAFFLES

MAKES 2 SERVINGS

1 cup pancake
   baking mix

⅔ cup milk

1 tablespoon
   vegetable oil

1 egg white

Juice of 1 lemon

2 tablespoons
   butter, melted

⅓ cup powdered
   sugar

⅔ cup assorted fresh
   berries or frozen
   berries, thawed

1. Preheat waffle maker to medium; lightly coat with nonstick cooking spray.

2. Whisk baking mix, milk, oil and egg white in large bowl. Scoop ¾ cup* mixture onto waffle maker, close and cook 4 minutes or until puffed and golden brown.

3. Remove to plate; repeat with remaining batter. Cut each waffle into portions. Place on serving platter.

4. Squeeze lemon juice over waffles. Drizzle with melted butter; sift powdered sugar and spoon berries on top.

*To make irregular-shaped waffles, reduce mixture to ¼ to ½ cup.

WAFFLES WITH STRAWBERRY SAUCE

MAKES ABOUT 6 ROUND WAFFLES

2¼ cups all-purpose flour

2 tablespoons sugar

1 tablespoon baking powder

½ teaspoon salt

2 eggs, beaten

¼ cup vegetable oil

2 cups milk

Strawberry Sauce (recipe follows)

1. Preheat waffle maker; grease lightly.

2. Sift flour, sugar, baking powder and salt into large bowl. Combine eggs, oil and milk in medium bowl. Stir liquid ingredients into dry ingredients until moistened.

3. For each waffle, pour about ¾ cup batter into waffle maker. Close lid and bake until steaming stops. Serve with Strawberry Sauce.

STRAWBERRY SAUCE

MAKES 1½ CUPS

1 pint strawberries, hulled

2 to 3 tablespoons sugar

1 tablespoon strawberry- or orange-flavored liqueur (optional)

Combine strawberries, sugar and liqueur in blender or food processor. Cover; process until smooth.

MEALTIME MEDLEY

WAFFLED CHICKEN SALTIMBOCCA

MAKES 4 SERVINGS

4 **boneless skinless chicken breasts (about 4 ounces each)**

Kosher salt

Freshly ground black pepper

4 **large fresh sage leaves**

4 **slices prosciutto**

1 **tablespoon vegetable oil**

1. Preheat classic waffle maker to high heat.

2. Season chicken on both sides with salt and pepper. Place sage leaf in center of each chicken breast.

3. Working one chicken breast at a time, wrap one slice prosciutto around center third of chicken so it covers the leaf completely. Brush prosciutto-wrapped chicken on both sides with oil. Repeat with remaining chicken.

4. Place two of the prepared chicken breasts side-by-side on waffle maker; close lid. Cook about 5 minutes or until chicken is opaque and firm. Remove to plate; tent with foil to keep warm. Repeat with remaining chicken.

SOUTHWESTERN CHEDDAR JALAPEÑO CORNMEAL WAFFLES

MAKES 8 SERVINGS

- ¾ cup all-purpose flour
- 1¼ cups medium-grind yellow cornmeal
- 2 tablespoons sugar
- 2 teaspoons baking powder
- ½ teaspoon baking soda
- 1 teaspoon salt
- ¾ cup shredded sharp Cheddar cheese
- 1 jalapeño pepper,* sliced into thin rings
- 6 tablespoons unsalted butter, melted and slightly cooled
- 2 cups buttermilk
- 2 eggs

Jalapeño peppers can sting and irritate the skin, so wear rubber gloves when handling peppers and do not touch your eyes.

1. Preheat classic waffle maker to medium-high heat. Set wire rack on top of large baking sheet.

2. Whisk flour, cornmeal, sugar, baking powder, baking soda and salt in large bowl until combined. Fold in cheese and jalapeño pepper; set aside.

3. Combine butter, buttermilk and eggs in large bowl. Pour buttermilk mixture into flour mixture; stir until combined.

4. Pour ½ cup batter into center of waffle maker; close lid and cook 3 to 5 minutes or until golden brown and crisp. Remove to wire rack; keep warm. Repeat with remaining batter.

SERVING SUGGESTION: Serve with a bowl of chili. Or, reheat leftovers and serve with salsa and avocado.

SPANIKOPITA WAFFLES

MAKES 4 SERVINGS

1 bag (8 ounces) frozen chopped spinach

4 green onions, white and green parts, thinly sliced

2 teaspoons dried dill weed

⅔ cup crumbled feta cheese

¼ teaspoon kosher salt

¼ teaspoon black pepper

¼ teaspoon ground nutmeg

1 package (17.3 ounces) puff pastry sheets, thawed

1. Bring large saucepan water to boil over high heat. Add spinach; bring to a boil. Boil 1 minute. Drain in colander using back of spoon to squeeze out as much liquid as possible. Transfer spinach to large bowl; cool 10 minutes.

2. Add green onions, dill, feta cheese, salt, pepper and nutmeg to spinach; stir well to combine.

3. Preheat Belgian waffle maker to medium-high heat. Place wire rack on top of large baking sheet.

4. Place one puff pastry sheet on lightly-floured work surface; cut in half. Roll out to size of waffle maker. Top one puff pastry piece with half of spinach mixture to within ½ inch of edge. Brush border with water; cover with other rolled half. Press edges together to seal; use fork to crimp edges.

5. Carefully move filled dough to waffle maker. Close lid gently; cook about 6 minutes or until pastry is browned and crisp. Remove to wire rack; keep warm. Repeat with remaining pastry and filling.

CRAB CAKE WAFFLES WITH GARLIC DIPPING SAUCE

MAKES 2 SERVINGS

8 ounces crabmeat

¼ cup finely chopped red bell pepper

½ teaspoon seafood seasoning

1 jalapeño pepper,* seeded and finely chopped

¼ cup mayonnaise

1 egg white

1 cup plain panko bread crumbs, divided

GARLIC DIPPING SAUCE

2 tablespoons mayonnaise

2 tablespoons sour cream

1 small clove garlic, minced

Black pepper

1 medium lemon, cut into wedges

Jalapeño peppers can sting and irritate the skin, so wear rubber gloves when handling peppers and do not touch your eyes.

1. Gently combine crabmeat, bell pepper, seafood seasoning, jalapeño pepper, ¼ cup mayonnaise, egg white and ⅓ cup bread crumbs in large bowl. Let stand 10 minutes.

2. Preheat waffle maker to medium; coat with nonstick cooking spray.

3. Place remaining ⅔ cup bread crumbs in shallow pie pan.

4. Combine 2 tablespoons mayonnaise, sour cream and garlic in small bowl; stir until combined. Sprinkle with black pepper.

5. Shape crab mixture into 4 patties; coat both sides with bread crumbs. Cook in waffle maker 4 minutes or until golden brown. Carefully remove to plate; keep warm. Repeat with remaining mixture. Serve with dipping sauce and lemon wedges.

NOTE: If crab cakes are too "loose" while assembling, add 1 to 2 tablespoons additional bread crumbs to mixture before shaping into patties.

WAFFLED BREAKFAST HASH WITH SMOKED TROUT

MAKES 4 SERVINGS

1¼ **pounds russet potatoes, peeled and cut into ½-inch pieces**

½ **small red onion, finely diced**

1 **small red bell pepper, seeded and cut into ½-inch pieces**

¼ **cup flaked smoked trout**

⅓ **cup sliced green onions, cut thinly on the bias**

2 **tablespoons vegetable oil**

1 **egg, lightly beaten**

2 **teaspoons cornstarch**

½ **teaspoon kosher salt**

¼ **teaspoon black pepper**

4 **fried eggs, for serving**

1. Preheat classic waffle maker to medium-high heat. Set wire rack on top of large baking sheet.

2. Place potatoes in large saucepan filled with enough water to cover potatoes by 1 inch. Heat to boil over high heat; reduce heat to medium-low and simmer, partially covered, 6 to 8 minutes or until tender. Drain potatoes in colander; rinse with cold running water.

3. Place potatoes, onion, bell pepper, trout, green onions, oil, beaten egg, cornstarch, salt and black pepper in large bowl; mix to combine.

4. Place 1 cup potato mixture in center of waffle maker. Close lid firmly; cook about 5 minutes or until waffle is golden brown and crisp. Remove to wire rack; tent with foil to keep warm. Repeat with remaining potato mixture.

5. Serve hash with fried eggs.

KOREAN SCALLION PANCAKE WAFFLES

MAKES 4 SERVINGS

DIPPING SAUCE

- **3** tablespoons low-sodium soy sauce
- **1½** tablespoons water
- **2** teaspoons rice vinegar
- **2** teaspoons sesame oil
- **¾** teaspoon sugar
- **1½** teaspoons sesame seeds
- **½** teaspoon minced garlic

WAFFLES

- **½** cup cornstarch
- **¾** cup all-purpose flour
- **½** teaspoon salt
- **1** cup ice cold water
- **1** egg, lightly beaten
- **½** red bell pepper, julienned into 2-inch pieces
- **¾** cup thinly sliced green onion, cut on the bias into 2-inch lengths
- **2** small carrots, peeled and grated (about ¾ cup)
- **2** teaspoons minced garlic
- **2** teaspoons vegetable oil, plus additional for brushing

1. Preheat classic waffle maker to medium-high heat. Set wire rack on top of large baking sheet.

2. Prepare dipping sauce. Whisk soy sauce, water, vinegar, sesame oil, sugar, sesame seeds and ½ teaspoon garlic in small bowl. Set aside.

3. Prepare waffles. Combine cornstarch, flour and salt in large bowl. Whisk in water and egg until combined. Fold in bell pepper, green onions, carrots and 2 teaspoons garlic.

4. Brush cooking grids of waffle maker with oil. Pour ½ cup batter in center of waffle maker and, using rubber spatula, gently spread batter so it covers entire surface of grid. Close lid; cook 2 minutes. Open lid; drizzle ½ teaspoon oil over top of waffle; close lid and continue cooking 4 to 5 minutes or until golden brown and crisp.

5. Remove waffles to wire rack; keep warm. Repeat with remaining batter, brushing waffle maker with oil before each batch.

6. Serve warm with dipping sauce.

PARMESAN EGGPLANT ROUNDS

MAKES 2 TO 4 SERVINGS

1 small eggplant (about 8 ounces), cut into ¾-inch rounds

½ cup olive oil and vinegar salad dressing

½ cup panko bread crumbs

2 tablespoons grated Parmesan cheese, plus additional for garnish

½ cup marinara sauce

2 tablespoons chopped fresh basil

Salt and black pepper

1. Preheat waffle maker to medium. Coat with nonstick cooking spray.

2. Brush both sides of eggplant with salad dressing.

3. Combine bread crumbs and 2 tablespoons cheese in shallow pie pan. Working in 2 batches, coat both sides of eggplant with bread crumbs, pressing down lightly to adhere. Place eggplant on bottom of waffle maker. Close, press down lightly, and cook 4 minutes or until golden brown. Remove to plate; keep warm. Repeat with remaining eggplant.

4. Place marinara sauce in small microwave-safe bowl. Cover; microwave on HIGH 20 seconds or until heated.

5. Top each eggplant piece with 1 tablespoon sauce. Sprinkle with basil, salt, pepper and additional cheese.

CHICKEN AND WAFFLES WITH SRIRACHA MAPLE SYRUP

MAKES 4 TO 6 SERVINGS

CHICKEN

- ½ **cup milk**
- 1 **egg**
- 1¼ **pounds chicken tenderloin, about 8 pieces**
- 1½ **cups panko bread crumbs**
- 1 **teaspoon paprika**
- 1 **teaspoon garlic powder**
- 1 **teaspoon salt**
- ½ **teaspoon black pepper**
- ¼ **cup vegetable oil**

WAFFLES

- 2 **cups baking mix**
- 1⅓ **cups milk**
- 1 **egg**

SRIRACHA MAPLE SYRUP

- ½ **cup pure maple syrup**
- 2 **teaspoons sriracha hot sauce**

1. Whish ½ cup milk and 1 egg in medium bowl. Add chicken; toss until well coated.

2. Combine bread crumbs, paprika, garlic powder, salt and pepper in shallow pie pan. Coat chicken, one at a time, in bread crumb mixture, pressing down lightly to allow crumbs to adhere. Remove to plate.

3. Heat oil in large nonstick skillet over medium-high heat. Reduce heat to medium; cook chicken 6 minutes on each side or until golden brown and no longer pink in center. Remove to plate; keep warm.

4. Preheat waffle maker to medium; coat with nonstick cooking spray. Combine waffle ingredients in medium bowl. Pour ¾ cup batter in waffle maker; cook 3 minutes or until golden brown. Remove to serving plate. Repeat with remaining batter.

5. Stir syrup and hot sauce in small bowl.

6. Top waffles with chicken tenders. Drizzle syrup on top.

TIPS: **If desired, top each waffle with 1 tablespoon melted butter before topping with chicken and syrup.**

For a super quick meal, use store-bought fried chicken tenders.

WEEKNIGHT WAFFLE-WICHES

MAKES 6 BELGIAN-STYLE WAFFLE SANDWICHES

PREP TIME: 10 minutes   COOKING TIME: 15 minutes

12 slices turkey bacon, cooked, *divided*

6 slices thinly-sliced deli ham (about 4 ounces), *divided*

1 can (12 fluid ounces) NESTLÉ® CARNATION® Evaporated Milk, *divided*

1 package (8 ounces) shredded cheddar cheese, *divided*

3 cups plus 1 teaspoon all-purpose baking mix (such as BISQUICK®), *divided*

¾ cup water

1 large egg, beaten

3 tablespoons prepared yellow mustard

COMBINE *¾ cup* evaporated milk, *1½ cups* cheese and *1 teaspoon* baking mix in small saucepan. Cook over medium heat, stirring constantly, until cheese is melted and sauce has slightly thickened to a creamy consistency. Remove from heat; cover.

WHISK together *remaining* evaporated milk, water, *remaining ½ cup* cheese, egg and mustard in medium bowl. Stir *remaining 3 cups* baking mix into milk mixture until well blended.

PREHEAT Belgian waffle maker* according to manufacturer's directions. Pour about *1¼ cups* batter onto waffle maker. (This amount is enough for a square or round waffle maker.) Cook according to manufacturer's directions. Repeat with remaining batter. Keep cooked waffles warm in oven.

*Can also be cooked in a standard waffle maker (makes about 8 standard-size waffles).

TO ASSEMBLE:

SPREAD *2 tablespoons* cheese sauce evenly over one side of 6 waffle squares. Place *2 slices* of bacon and *1 slice* of ham on cheese sauce on each. Top with second waffle to make waffle-wiches.

TIP: **Waffles can be made ahead and frozen.**

SCRAMBLED EGG PILE UPS

MAKES 1 SERVING

2 eggs

2 tablespoons milk

Salt and black pepper

¼ cup diced orange bell pepper

1 whole green onion, thinly sliced

¼ cup grape tomatoes, quartered (about 6 tomatoes)

⅓ cup (about 1½ ounces) shredded Cheddar cheese

1 to 2 tablespoons sour cream (optional)

1. Preheat waffle maker to medium; coat with nonstick cooking spray.

2. Whisk eggs and milk in small bowl. Season lightly with salt and black pepper. Working quickly, pour egg mixture onto waffle maker, sprinkle with bell pepper, green onion and tomatoes. Close; cook 2 minutes or until puffed.

3. Remove "waffle" to plate; sprinkle with cheese and top with sour cream, if desired. Serve immediately.

TIP: To remove from waffle maker, place a plate over the egg and flip the egg onto the plate. Or, use the tip of a fork to gently release egg from waffle maker, then slide a wide spatula under to gently remove.

SERVING SUGGESTION: For a hearty breakfast, serve with hash brown potatoes and bacon.

WAFFLED PANKO MAC AND CHEESE

MAKES 2 SERVINGS

- 4 ounces uncooked elbow macaroni (about 1 cup)
- 4 slices American cheese
- 1 tablespoon butter
- 1 teaspoon Dijon mustard
- Salt and black pepper (optional)
- 1 egg white
- ½ cup plain panko bread crumbs
- 4 teaspoons extra virgin olive oil
- 1 tablespoon chopped fresh parsley *or* 1 whole green onion, chopped

1. Prepare macaroni in large saucepan according to package directions. Drain; return to saucepan.

2. Place saucepan over low heat; add cheese, butter and mustard. Stir until cheese melts. Season with salt and pepper, if desired.

3. Place macaroni and cheese mixture in shallow pie pan; let cool slightly. Spread in even layer; refrigerate to cool completely, about 30 minutes.

4. Preheat waffle maker to medium-high heat; coat with nonstick cooking spray.

5. Add egg white and bread crumbs to cooled macaroni mixture. Spoon ½ mixture onto waffle maker; close, press down lightly. Cook 4 minutes or until browned and slightly crisp. Gently remove using fork and spatula.

6. Repeat with remaining macaroni mixture. Sprinkle lightly with salt and pepper, if desired. Drizzle with oil and sprinkle with parsley before serving.

TIPS: For smaller portions, prepare four small waffles instead of two.

A great way to use up leftover macaroni and cheese! Just add egg white and bread crumbs and go from there.

Delicious for breakfast too!

APPLE-SAGE BREAKFAST SAUSAGE

MAKES 3 TO 4 SERVINGS

- 1 **pound ground pork**
- ¼ **cup applesauce**
- 1 **tablespoon maple syrup**
- 1½ **teaspoons kosher salt**
- ½ **teaspoon black pepper**
- 1 **teaspoon minced fresh sage**
- 1 **teaspoon minced garlic**
- ¼ **teaspoon ground nutmeg**

1. Preheat classic waffle maker to medium-high heat.

2. Combine all ingredients in large bowl; mix well. Spoon about ¼ cup mixture into hand; roll into balls, making about 6 to 8 balls total. Place on large plate; slightly flatten each ball into patties.

3. Working in batches, place patties on waffle maker; close lightly. Cook about 3 minutes or until dark brown waffle marks appear and sausages are cooked through. Remove to plate; tent with foil to keep warm. Repeat with remaining patties, wiping grids with paper towels as needed to absorb excess fat.

SERVING SUGGESTION: Serve with scrambled eggs and fresh fruit.

WAFFLES BENEDICT

MAKES 8 SERVINGS

PREP TIME: 10 minutes   COOKING TIME: 10 minutes

1 can (12 fluid ounces) NESTLÉ® CARNATION® Evaporated Milk

1½ cups (6 ounces) shredded cheddar cheese

1 teaspoon all-purpose flour

8 frozen toaster waffles

8 large eggs, well-beaten

½ teaspoon salt

¼ teaspoon ground black pepper

Nonstick cooking spray

8 slices bacon, cooked and crumbled

Chopped chives (optional)

COMBINE ¾ *cup* evaporated milk, cheese and flour in small saucepan. Cook over medium heat, stirring constantly, for about 3 minutes or until cheese is melted and sauce has slightly thickened to a creamy consistency. Remove from heat; cover.

TOAST waffles according to package directions. Keep warm.

WHISK together *remaining* evaporated milk, eggs, salt and pepper in medium bowl. Spray large skillet with nonstick cooking spray; heat over medium heat. Pour egg mixture into skillet. Cook, stirring frequently, until eggs are cooked.

TO ASSEMBLE:

TOP each waffle with eggs, cheese sauce, bacon and chives.

CRUNCHY HASH BROWN WAFFLES

MAKES 4 WAFFLES (8 SERVINGS)

- **4 cups finely shredded potatoes**
- **½ cup finely diced onion**
- **1 egg**
- **¼ cup all-purpose flour**
- **2 tablespoons vegetable oil**
- **1 teaspoon salt**
- **Black pepper**

1. Preheat waffle maker to medium-high. Combine potatoes, onion, egg, flour, oil and salt in large bowl. Season with pepper; mix well.

2. Scoop 1 cup potato mixture onto waffle maker. Carefully spread to cover surface. Close and cook about 8 minutes or until golden brown and crisp.

NOTE: Serve these with ketchup, sour cream, crumbled bacon, shredded cheese, or applesauce. They would be equally delicious for brunch or served as a side with roasted chicken or fish.

FUN FOODS

MONKEY WAFFLE BITES

MAKES 4 SERVINGS

1 can (8 ounces) refrigerated crescent dough, without seams preferred

½ cup plus 2 tablespoons chocolate hazelnut spread, divided

¼ cup sliced almonds, divided

1 banana, thinly sliced

1. Roll out dough onto cutting board. Spread ½ cup chocolate spread over top of dough, leaving ½-inch border around the edge. Sprinkle with 2 tablespoons almonds. Roll up dough into log. Refrigerate 1 to 2 hours.

2. Preheat waffle maker to medium. Cut log into four 2-inch-wide slices. Place slices, cut-side down, in waffle maker. Close and cook, about 5 minutes, until cooked through and golden brown. Continue with remaining slices.

3. Place 2 tablespoons chocolate spread in small microwave-safe bowl. Heat in microwave on HIGH 20 to 30 seconds until heated through.

4. Top each waffle with banana slices; drizzle with chocolate and 2 tablespoons almonds.

WAFFLED BURGER SLIDERS

MAKES 8 SLIDERS

½ **pound lean ground beef**

½ **teaspoon salt**

Black pepper

4 **slider buns** *or* **4 slices bread, cut into quarters**

1 **tablespoon butter, melted**

Desired toppings (lettuce, tomatoes, cheese, pickles, ketchup)

1. Combine beef and salt in large bowl. Season with pepper. Divide into 8 small patties; set aside.

2. Heat waffle maker to medium. Brush buns with melted butter; set aside.

3. Place 4 patties at a time in waffle maker. Cook, about 3 minutes, or until cooked through. Place 1 patty in each bun, adding desired toppings.

PEPPERONI PIZZA DIPPERS

MAKES 4 SERVINGS

1 can (8 ounces) refrigerated crescent dough, without seams preferred

2 tablespoons marinara sauce, plus additional for dipping

4 tablespoons shredded mozzarella cheese, divided

8 slices pepperoni, divided

1. Preheat waffle maker to medium. Carefully unroll dough onto cutting board. Cut into 4 rectangles.

2. Place one rectangle onto waffle maker. Top with 1 tablespoon sauce, leaving ½-inch boarder around edge; 1 tablespoon cheese; 4 slices pepperoni and 1 tablespoon cheese. Carefully top with another dough rectangle. Close waffle maker.

3. Cook about 8 minutes, or until dough is cooked through and golden brown. Repeat with remaining dough, sauce, cheese and pepperoni.

4. Cut as desired; serve with additional sauce.

LEMON RAMEN WAFFLES

MAKES 6 SERVINGS

3 packages
   (3 ounces each)
   ramen noodles,
   any flavor*

1 cup all-purpose
   flour

3 tablespoons sugar

½ teaspoon baking
   powder

¼ teaspoon baking
   soda

½ teaspoon salt

1 cup buttermilk

1 egg

1 egg yolk

1 teaspoon grated
   lemon peel

1½ tablespoons
   lemon juice

½ teaspoon vanilla

*Discard seasoning
packets.*

1. Preheat waffle maker to medium; coat with nonstick cooking spray.

2. Prepare noodles according to package directions, cooking 2 minutes until slightly firm (al dente). Drain.

3. Combine flour, sugar, baking powder, baking soda and salt in medium bowl; set aside.

4. Combine buttermilk, egg, egg yolk, lemon peel, lemon juice and vanilla in medium bowl; stir until well blended. Stir buttermilk mixture into flour mixture until just blended.

5. Place ½ cup noodles on waffle maker. Spoon ¼ cup batter evenly over noodles. Cook in waffle maker according to manufacturer's directions.

6. Remove waffle to plate; keep warm. Repeat with remaining noodles and batter.

TIP: You may want to place cooked waffles in warmed (170°F) oven while cooking remaining waffles.

TOPPING SUGGESTIONS: Powdered sugar, fresh fruits, yogurt, sour cream, almonds—all make great toppings for your waffles.

CINNAMON SWEET BAGELETTES

MAKES 1 SERVING

2 tablespoons
   butter, softened

2 tablespoons
   packed light
   brown sugar

1 teaspoon ground
   cinnamon

1 plain bagel, split

1. Preheat waffle maker to medium; lightly coat with nonstick cooking spray.

2. Combine butter, brown sugar and cinnamon in small bowl. Place bagel halves in waffle maker, close, press down to flatten slightly; cook 2 minutes or until lightly golden. Remove to plate.

3. Top with butter mixture. Serve warm.

TIP: **You can also try mini bagels for a fun snack.**

PANINI WAFFLINI

MAKES 2 SERVINGS

2 tablespoons extra
   virgin olive oil

4 slices Italian
   bread

2 ounces fresh
   mozzarella
   cheese, cut
   into slices *or*
   ½ cup shredded
   mozzarella
   cheese

2 plum tomatoes,
   sliced

4 fresh basil leaves

8 pitted kalamata
   olives, cut in half

1. Preheat waffle maker to medium.

2. Brush oil on both sides of bread slices. Top two slices bread with cheese, tomatoes, basil, olives and remaining bread slices.

3. Place sandwiches, one at a time, in waffle maker; close while pressing down slightly. Cook 2 minutes or until golden brown and cheese has melted.

QUICK WAFFLED QUESADILLAS

MAKES 1 SERVING

2 (6-inch) flour tortillas

⅓ cup (1½ ounces) shredded Cheddar cheese or Monterey Jack cheese

¼ cup finely chopped poblano pepper or jalapeño pepper*

1 small plum tomato, chopped

⅛ teaspoon ground cumin

Salt and black pepper

½ ripe medium avocado, chopped

1 to 2 tablespoons chopped fresh cilantro

Juice of ½ lime

*Jalapeño and poblano peppers can sting and irritate the skin, so wear rubber gloves when handling peppers and do not touch your eyes.

1. Preheat waffle maker to medium; coat both sides of each tortilla with nonstick cooking spray.

2. Top tortilla with cheese, poblano pepper, tomato, cumin, salt, black pepper and other tortilla. Place on waffle maker; close, pressing down slightly. Cook 3 minutes or until golden brown and cheese has melted.

3. Carefully remove tortilla. Cut into four sections, using a serrated knife. Top with avocado, cilantro and lime juice.

TIPS: If cheese runs over, let waffle maker cool to easily remove cheese.

Squeeze lime juice from remaining half of lime over remaining avocado; cover and store in refrigerator for another use.

GARLIC BREAD WAFFLE STICKS

MAKES 5 TO 6 SERVINGS

2 cloves garlic, minced

¼ teaspoon kosher salt

3 tablespoons unsalted butter, melted

2 tablespoons finely chopped fresh parsley

¼ cup grated Parmesan cheese

2 cans (8 ounces each) refrigerated crescent dough

Marinara sauce (for dipping)

1. Preheat classic square waffle maker to medium-high heat. Set wire rack on top of large baking sheet.

2. Place garlic on cutting board; sprinkle with salt. Using tip of chef's knife, press salt into garlic until it forms smooth paste. Transfer paste to medium bowl; stir in butter, parsley and cheese.

3. Unroll dough. Arrange dough edge-to-edge onto waffle maker to fill entire cooking surface, cutting pieces as needed to fit.

4. Close lid; cook about 2 minutes or until golden brown. Open lid; brush top of waffle with garlic butter. Close lid; cook 30 seconds. Remove to wire rack. Repeat with remaining dough.

5. Cut into sticks. Serve with marinara sauce.

WAFFLED FRENCH TOAST

MAKES 2 TO 3 SERVINGS

1 cup milk

2 eggs

2 tablespoons honey

2 teaspoons vanilla

1 teaspoon ground cinnamon

8 slices thick-sliced bread

Maple syrup, powdered sugar and butter (optional)

1. Combine milk, eggs, honey, vanilla and cinnamon in shallow bowl or pie pan. Dip bread, one slice at a time, in mixture letting bread soak up the liquid.

2. Preheat waffle maker to medium. Cook bread, one slice at a time, about 4 minutes or until golden brown and crisp. Keep warm on plate tented with foil until all bread is cooked.

3. Serve with maple syrup, powdered sugar and butter, as desired.

CINNAMON-SUGAR CAKE DONUT WAFFLES

MAKES 6 SERVINGS

¾ cup sugar

1½ teaspoons ground nutmeg

2 teaspoons ground cinnamon

1¼ cups all-purpose flour

½ cup whole wheat flour

½ teaspoon salt

2 teaspoons baking powder

1¾ cups buttermilk

2 eggs

6 tablespoons unsalted butter, melted and slightly cooled

1½ teaspoons vanilla

1. Preheat classic waffle maker to medium-high heat. Place wire rack on top of large baking sheet.

2. Combine sugar, nutmeg and cinnamon in small bowl. Set aside ½ cup sugar mixture in large bowl; place remainder in large resealable food storage bag.

3. Add flours, salt and baking powder to ½ cup sugar mixture in large bowl. Combine buttermilk, eggs, butter and vanilla; stir into dry ingredients until just combined.

4. Place scant ¾ cup batter in center of waffle maker. Close lid and cook 3 to 5 minutes or until waffle is golden brown. Remove waffle and place in storage bag; seal and shake until evenly coated. Remove to wire rack; keep warm. Repeat with remaining batter.

WAFFLED GRILLED CHEESE

MAKES 1 SERVING

2 tablespoons
  butter

2 slices bread

1 teaspoon mustard

1 slice American
  cheese

1 slice ham

1. Preheat waffle maker to medium. Spread 1 tablespoon butter on one side of each bread slice; spread mustard on other side. Layer cheese and ham over mustard. Top with remaining bread slice, mustard side down.

2. Coat waffle maker lightly with nonstick cooking spray. Place sandwich in waffle maker; close lid. Cook 3 to 5 minutes or until top is browned and cheese is melted.

LEFTOVERS ANYONE?

CHEESY MASHED POTATO WAFFLES

MAKES 3 SERVINGS

- 2 cups pre-made or leftover mashed potatoes
- 1 cup (4 ounces) shredded Cheddar cheese
- ¼ cup chopped green onions
- ⅓ cup buttermilk
- 2 eggs
- 2 tablespoons butter, melted
- ½ cup all-purpose flour
- 1 teaspoon baking powder
- ½ teaspoon salt

1. Preheat waffle maker to medium.

2. Combine potatoes, cheese, green onions, buttermilk, eggs, melted butter, flour, baking powder and salt in large bowl; stir well.

3. Scoop 1 cup potato mixture onto waffle maker; spread to cover. Cook about 5 minutes or until golden brown and crisp.

SERVING SUGGESTION: Serve garnished with a dollop of sour cream, shredded cheese and bacon bits.

BLT WAFFLE-WICHES

MAKES 2 SANDWICHES

4 leftover waffles
   or Buttermilk
   Waffles (recipe
   follows)

2 tablespoons
   mayonnaise

4 slices cooked
   bacon

1 tomato, sliced
   into 4 slices

2 lettuce leaves

Spread mayonnaise on waffles.
Add 2 slices bacon, 2 slices tomato
and lettuce to two waffles.
Top with remaining waffles; cut
in half or fold over large waffle to
create sandwich.

BUTTERMILK WAFFLES

MAKES 6 WAFFLES

1½ cups all-purpose
    flour

¼ cup cornstarch

2 tablespoons sugar

2 teaspoons baking
   powder

½ teaspoon baking
   soda

1¼ cups buttermilk

2 eggs

¼ cup (½ stick)
   butter, melted

1 teaspoon vanilla

1. Preheat waffle maker to medium.
Combine flour, cornstarch, sugar,
baking powder and baking soda
in large bowl. Stir in buttermilk,
eggs, melted butter and vanilla until
combined.

2. Scoop ¾ cup batter onto waffle
maker. Cook until golden brown
and crisp. (Follow manufacturer's
direction for timing.)

TIP: Whenever you have leftover
waffles, wrap them individually and
freeze. They can easily be reheated
for a quick breakfast or are great for
sandwiches.

TURKEY BACON MINI WAFFLEWICHES

MAKES 2 SERVINGS

1 teaspoon Dijon mustard

1 teaspoon honey

2 leftover waffles, cut into 4 pieces each *or* 8 frozen mini waffles

2 thin slices deli turkey, cut into thin strips

2 tablespoons cooked and crumbled bacon

4 teaspoons shredded Cheddar or mozzarella cheese

2 teaspoons butter

1. Combine mustard and honey in small bowl. Spread small amount of mustard mixture onto one side of four waffle pieces. Top evenly with turkey and bacon; sprinkle with cheese. Top with remaining waffle pieces.

2. Melt butter in medium nonstick skillet over medium heat. Pressing with back of spatula, cook sandwiches 3 to 4 minutes per side or until cheese melts and waffles are golden brown.

FRUITED WAFFLE PARFAIT CUP

MAKES 4 SERVINGS

1 cooked or leftover Belgian waffle, torn into bite-sized pieces

½ cup raspberry jam

½ teaspoon almond extract

1 cup plain or vanilla yogurt

2 cups chopped fresh peaches or frozen peaches, thawed

1. Place equal amounts of waffle pieces in each of four parfait dishes.

2. Place jam in small microwave-safe bowl; microwave on HIGH 30 seconds to slightly melt. Stir in extract until smooth. Spoon over waffle; top with yogurt and fruit.

TIPS: Great with ice cream or frozen yogurt for dessert.
What a great use for leftover waffles!

STRAWBERRY-TOPPED WAFFLES WITH SWEET AND CREAMY SAUCE

MAKES 4 SERVINGS

3 ounces cream cheese

¼ cup half-and-half

1 tablespoon sugar

¼ teaspoon vanilla

4 frozen leftover waffles

1 cup sliced fresh strawberries

1. Combine cream cheese, half-and-half, sugar and vanilla in blender; blend until smooth.

2. Toast waffles. Spoon sauce over waffles; top with strawberries.

HOT FUDGE WAFFLE SUNDAES

MAKES 3 TO 4 SERVINGS

3 leftover waffles,
  cut into 4 pieces
  each *or* 12 frozen
  mini waffles

2 tablespoons hot
  fudge topping

¾ cup Neapolitan
  ice cream

4 tablespoons
  whipped cream

  Colored sprinkles
  (optional)

1. Heat waffles in toaster until lightly browned. Heat hot fudge topping in microwave according to package directions.

2. Arrange waffles on serving plates. Top with ice cream. Evenly drizzle hot fudge topping over top; garnish with whipped cream and sprinkles, if desired.

HAM & EGG MINI WAFFLEWICHES

MAKES 2 SERVINGS (2 WAFFLEWICHES EACH)

1 **egg, lightly beaten**

2 **leftover waffles, cut into 4 pieces each** *or* **8 frozen mini waffles**

2 **teaspoons butter**

2 **thin slices deli ham (about 1 ounce each), cut in half**

4 **teaspoons shredded Cheddar cheese**

1. Spray small skillet with nonstick cooking spray; heat over medium heat. Pour egg into skillet; cook and stir until set.

2. Spread one side of each waffle with butter. Place ham slice on unbuttered side. Top each evenly with cooked egg and cheese. Top with remaining waffles, buttered side up.

3. Heat medium skillet over medium heat. Pressing with back of spatula, cook sandwiches 4 minutes per side or until cheese melts and waffles are golden brown.

WAFFLES WITH SWEET STRAWBERRIES

MAKES 4 SERVINGS

1 cup sliced fresh
   strawberries

½ tablespoon sugar
   substitute*

2 tablespoons
   orange juice

½ teaspoon grated
   orange peel
   (optional)

4 leftover waffles,
   cut into
   4 pieces each
   or 16 frozen
   mini waffles

¼ cup light sour
   cream

*This recipe was tested
with sucralose-based sugar
substitute.*

1. Combine strawberries, sugar substitute, orange juice and orange peel, if desired, in medium bowl. Toss gently, yet thoroughly, to blend. Let stand 20 minutes.

2. Heat waffles in toaster until lightly browned. Place four waffle pieces on serving plates. Top each serving with 1 tablespoon sour cream. Spoon ¼ cup berry mixture evenly around sour cream.

DOUBLY DESSERTS

CHOCOLATE CHIP ICE CREAM SANDWICHES

MAKES 4 SERVINGS

1 cup packaged dry waffle mix

⅔ cup milk

1 egg

1 tablespoon vegetable oil

⅔ cup mini semisweet chocolate chips

2 cups favorite flavor ice cream

Assorted sprinkles, mini semisweet chocolate chips (optional)

1. Preheat waffle maker to medium. Combine waffle mix, milk, egg oil and ⅔ cup chocolate chips in large bowl.

2. Scoop 1 cup batter onto waffle maker; cook until golden brown and crisp. Repeat with remaining batter. Cool slightly.

3. Cut waffles into 4 segments each. Top with ½ cup ice cream and another waffle to make sandwich. Roll sides in sprinkles or chocolate chips, if desired. Wrap in foil and freeze 1 hour or until firm.

CARROT CAKE WAFFLES WITH CREAM CHEESE DRIZZLE

MAKES 4 SERVINGS

WAFFLES

- 1 **cup packaged dry waffle mix**
- 1 **cup milk**
- 1 **egg**
- 2 **tablespoons vegetable oil**
- 1 **teaspoon ground cinnamon**
- 1 **cup shredded carrots**
- ⅓ **cup raisins**

CREAM CHEESE DRIZZLE

- 4 **ounces cream cheese, softened**
- ½ **stick (4 ounces) butter, softened**
- 1½ **cups powdered sugar**
- ¼ **cup milk**
- 1 **teaspoon vanilla**

1. Combine waffle mix, 1 cup milk, egg, oil and cinnamon in large bowl; mix well. Fold in carrots and raisins.

2. Preheat waffle maker to medium. Spoon ½ to 1 cup batter into waffle maker; cook until golden brown and crisp.

3. Beat cream cheese, butter, powdered sugar, ¼ cup milk and vanilla in large bowl of electric mixer. Drizzle over waffles to serve.

S'MORES WAFFLES

MAKES 4 TO 6 SERVINGS

1 cup whole wheat flour

¾ cup finely ground graham cracker crumbs

½ teaspoon salt

2 teaspoons baking powder

½ cup mini chocolate chips, plus additional for serving

8 tablespoons (1 stick) unsalted butter, melted and slightly cooled

1¼ cups milk

2 eggs

¼ cup honey

1 teaspoon vanilla

MARSHMALLOW SAUCE

1 tablespoon unsalted butter

2 cups miniature marshmallows

1. Preheat Belgian waffle maker to medium-high to high heat. Set wire rack on top of large baking sheet.

2. Combine flour, graham cracker crumbs, salt and baking powder in large bowl. Stir in ½ cup chocolate chips.

3. Combine 8 tablespoons butter, milk, eggs, honey and vanilla in large bowl. Pour over dry ingredients; stir to combine.

4. Pour ⅓ cup batter into each well of waffle maker. Close lid; cook 5 to 8 minutes or until waffles are lightly browned. Remove to wire rack; keep warm. Repeat with remaining batter.

5. While waffles are cooking, prepare marshmallow sauce. Melt 1 tablespoon butter in small saucepan over medium heat. Add marshmallows; cook 3 to 4 minutes, stirring occasionally, or until completely melted. Remove from heat; cover to keep warm.

6. Drizzle sauce and additional chocolate chips over waffles to serve.

CHOCOLATE DESSERT WAFFLES

MAKES ABOUT 10 (4-INCH) WAFFLES

½ cup HERSHEY'S® Cocoa

¼ cup (½ stick) butter or margarine, melted

¾ cup sugar

2 eggs

2 teaspoons vanilla extract

1 cup all-purpose flour

½ teaspoon baking soda

½ teaspoon salt

½ cup buttermilk or sour milk*

½ cup chopped nuts (optional)

HOT FUDGE SAUCE (recipe follows)

STRAWBERRY DESSERT CREAM or APPLE-CINNAMON TOPPING or PEACH-NUTMEG TOPPING or CHOCOLATE MAPLE SAUCE (recipes follow)

*To sour milk: Use 1½ teaspoons white vinegar plus milk to equal ½ cup.

1. Stir cocoa and butter in large bowl until smooth; stir in sugar. Add eggs and vanilla; beat well. Stir together flour, baking soda and salt; add alternately with buttermilk to cocoa mixture. Stir in nuts, if desired.

2. Bake in waffle iron according to manufacturer's directions. Carefully remove waffle from iron. Serve with desired toppings.

NOTE: Leftover waffles may be frozen; thaw in toaster on low heat.

STRAWBERRY DESSERT CREAM: Beat 1 cup (½ pint) cold whipping cream in small bowl until stiff. Fold in ⅓ cup strawberry preserves and 3 drops red food color, if desired. Makes about 2 cups topping.

APPLE–CINNAMON TOPPING: Heat 1 can (21 ounces) apple pie filling, 1 tablespoon butter or margarine and ⅛ teaspoon ground cinnamon in small saucepan until warm.

PEACH–NUTMEG TOPPING: Heat 1 can (21 ounces) peach pie filling and ⅛ teaspoon ground nutmeg in small saucepan until warm.

HOT FUDGE SAUCE

MAKES ABOUT 1¾ CUPS SAUCE

¾ cup sugar

½ cup HERSHEY'S® Cocoa

½ cup plus 2 tablespoons (5-ounce can) evaporated milk

⅓ cup light corn syrup

⅓ cup butter or margarine

1 teaspoon vanilla extract

Combine sugar and cocoa in small saucepan; stir in evaporated milk and corn syrup. Cook over medium heat, stirring constantly, until mixture boils; boil and stir 1 minute. Remove from heat. Add butter and vanilla; stirring until butter is melted. Serve warm.

CHOCOLATE MAPLE SAUCE

MAKES ABOUT 1⅓ CUPS SAUCE

¾ cup sugar

⅓ cup HERSHEY'S® Cocoa

¾ cup evaporated milk

¼ cup (½ stick) butter or margarine

⅛ teaspoon salt

½ teaspoon maple flavor

½ teaspoon vanilla extract

Combine sugar and cocoa in small saucepan; stir in evaporated milk. Cook over medium heat, stirring constantly, until mixture boils; boil and stir 1 minute. Remove from heat. Add butter and salt, stirring until butter is melted. Stir in maple flavor and vanilla. Serve warm. Refrigerate leftovers.

DESSERT WAFFLES

MAKES 14 (5×4-INCH) WAFFLES

- 1¾ cups all-purpose flour
- 1 tablespoon sugar
- 2 teaspoons baking powder
- ½ teaspoon salt
- 1½ cups nonfat milk
- 2 egg yolks
- ¼ cup Dried Plum Purée (recipe follows)
- 1 tablespoon vegetable oil
- 4 egg whites
- 2 pints fat free vanilla ice cream or frozen yogurt

Heat waffle iron. In large bowl, combine flour, sugar, baking powder and salt. In medium bowl, whisk milk, egg yolks, dried plum purée and oil until blended; mix into flour mixture just until blended. In mixer bowl, beat egg whites until soft peaks form. Immediately fold into batter. Bake waffles according to manufacturer's directions. Place waffles on individual plates and top each with generous ¼-cup scoop of ice cream. Serve with your choice of topping, if desired.

NOTE: Waffles can be made in advance and cooled, wrapped, frozen and reheated in a toaster or toaster oven.

SUGGESTED TOPPINGS: Fat free fudge and caramel sauces, strawberry and pineapple toppings, frozen or fresh seasonal fruit and low fat nondairy whipped topping.

DRIED PLUM PURÉE: Combine 1⅓ cups (8 ounces) pitted dried plums and 6 tablespoons hot water in container of food processor or blender. Pulse on and off until dried plums are finely chopped and smooth. Store leftovers in a covered container in the refrigerator for up to two months.

Courtesy of California Dried Plum Board

PUMPKIN WAFFLES WITH PUMPKIN "MARMALADE"

MAKES 10 WAFFLES AND 4 CUPS MARMALADE

1 can (29 ounces) solid-pack pumpkin, divided

1 cup packed brown sugar

1 cup water

1 cup orange juice

1 tablespoon maple syrup

1 teaspoon finely grated orange peel

½ teaspoon ground ginger

¼ teaspoon salt

1 package (about 15 ounces) yellow cake mix

2 teaspoons pumpkin pie spice

1½ cups milk

2 eggs

¼ cup (½ stick) butter, melted

Whipped cream (optional)

1. Preheat oven to 200°F. Place wire rack on top of baking sheet; place in oven.

2. Reserve 1 cup pumpkin; set aside for waffles. Combine remaining pumpkin, brown sugar, water, orange juice, maple syrup, orange peel, ginger and salt in medium saucepan; bring to a simmer over medium heat. Cook until mixture thickens to consistency of applesauce, stirring occasionally. Reduce heat to low; keep warm.

3. Combine cake mix and pumpkin pie spice in large bowl; mix well. Combine milk, reserved 1 cup pumpkin, eggs and butter in medium bowl until well blended. Add to dry ingredients; mix well.

4. Preheat waffle iron according to manufacturer's directions. Spray cooking surface with nonstick cooking spray.

5. Pour ½ cup batter into heated waffle iron. Cook until steaming stops and waffle is lightly browned and crisp. Remove to wire rack in oven to keep warm. Repeat with remaining batter. Serve with warm pumpkin marmalade and whipped cream, if desired. Refrigerate leftover marmalade.

BACON WAFFLES WITH MAPLE CREAM

MAKES 9 TO 10 WAFFLES

MAPLE CREAM

- 1 cup whipping cream
- ¼ cup maple syrup

WAFFLES

- 1 package (about 18 ounces) butter-recipe yellow cake mix
- 1¼ cups buttermilk*
- 3 large eggs
- ½ cup (1 stick) butter, melted and cooled
- ¼ cup maple syrup
- 1 pound maple bacon, cooked and diced (about 1¾ cups)**

If buttermilk is unavailable, substitute 3½ teaspoons vinegar or lemon juice and enough milk to equal 1¼ cups. Let stand 5 minutes.

**Also delicious with applewood-smoked bacon.*

1. Preheat oven to 200°F. Place wire rack on top of baking sheet; place in oven. Preheat waffle iron according to manufacturer's directions. Spray cooking surface with nonstick cooking spray.

2. Beat whipping cream and ¼ cup maple syrup in chilled medium bowl with electric mixer at medium speed until soft peaks form. Refrigerate until ready to serve.

3. Combine cake mix, buttermilk, eggs, butter and ¼ cup maple syrup in large bowl. Add bacon; mix well. Spoon batter by ½ cupfuls onto heated waffle iron (batter will be thick). Cook 4 minutes or until steaming stops and waffles are lightly browned. Remove to wire rack in oven to keep warm. Repeat with remaining batter. Serve with chilled maple cream.

BANANA BREAD WAFFLES WITH CINNAMON BUTTER

MAKES 4 SERVINGS

½ cup unsalted whipped butter, softened

2 tablespoons powdered sugar

2 teaspoons grated orange peel

¼ teaspoon ground cinnamon

¼ teaspoon vanilla

1 package (7 ounces) banana muffin mix

⅔ cup buttermilk

1 egg

Maple syrup (optional)

1. Preheat waffle maker.

2. Combine butter, powdered sugar, orange peel, cinnamon and vanilla in small bowl; mix well. Set aside.

3. Combine muffin mix, buttermilk and egg in medium bowl; stir until just moistened.

4. Spray waffle maker with nonstick cooking spray. Spoon half of batter (1 cup) onto waffle maker and cook according to manufacturer's directions. Repeat with remaining batter.

5. Spoon equal amount of butter mixture onto each waffle just before serving. Lightly drizzle syrup over top, if desired.

PEACHES AND CREAMY DIP WITH WAFFLE WEDGES

MAKES 16 TO 24 WEDGES AND ABOUT ¾ CUP DIP

4 ounces (½ of an 8-ounce package) cream cheese

⅓ cup peach preserves

1 tablespoon milk

2 teaspoons sugar

½ teaspoon vanilla

4 frozen mini waffles *or* 4 small leftover frozen waffles

Ground cinnamon

1. Place cream cheese, preserves, milk, sugar and vanilla in blender container; blend until smooth. Set aside.

2. Heat waffles in toaster to lightly brown; cut each into 4 to 6 wedges.

3. Place cream cheese mixture in small serving bowl; sprinkle with cinnamon. Serve with waffle wedges for dipping.

CHOCOLATE BRUNCH WAFFLES

MAKES 10 BELGIAN WAFFLE SQUARES

PREP TIME: 10 minutes **COOKING TIME:** 12 minutes

2¼ cups all-purpose flour

½ cup granulated sugar

1 tablespoon baking powder

¾ teaspoon salt

1 cup (6 ounces) NESTLÉ® TOLL HOUSE® Semi-Sweet Chocolate Morsels

¾ cup (1½ sticks) butter or margarine

1½ cups milk

3 large eggs, lightly beaten

1 tablespoon vanilla extract

Toppings (whipped cream, chocolate shavings, sifted powdered sugar, fresh fruit, ice cream)

COMBINE flour, sugar, baking powder and salt in large bowl.

MICROWAVE morsels and butter in medium, uncovered, microwave-safe bowl on HIGH (100%) power for 1 minute. STIR. Morsels may retain some of their original shape. If necessary, microwave at additional 10- to 15-second intervals, stirring just until morsels are melted. Cool to room temperature. Stir in milk, eggs and vanilla extract. Add chocolate mixture to flour mixture; stir (batter will be thick).

COOK in Belgian waffle maker* according to manufacturer's directions. Serve warm with your choice of toppings.

Can also be cooked in standard waffle maker (makes about 20 standard-size waffle squares).

RED VELVET WAFFLES WITH BERRIES

MAKES ABOUT 10 WAFFLES
(DEPENDING ON SIZE OF WAFFLE PLATE)

- 2 quarts strawberries or other combination of berries
- 1¼ cups sugar, divided
- ¼ cup HERSHEY'S® Cocoa
- ¼ cup (½ stick) butter or margarine, melted
- 2 eggs
- 1 tablespoon red food color
- 2 teaspoons vanilla extract
- 1¼ cups all-purpose flour
- ½ teaspoon salt
- ¼ teaspoon baking soda
- ¼ teaspoon baking powder
- ½ cup buttermilk or sour milk*

  Sweetened whipped cream or whipped topping

  HERSHEY'S® Syrup (optional)

*To sour milk: Use 1½ teaspoons white vinegar plus milk to equal ½ cup.

1. Rinse, pat dry and slice strawberries into large bowl. Stir in ½ cup sugar; set aside while preparing waffles.

2. Stir cocoa and butter in bowl until smooth; stir in remaining ¾ cup sugar. Add eggs, food color and vanilla; beat well. Stir together flour, salt, baking soda and baking powder; add alternately with buttermilk to cocoa mixture.

3. Bake in waffle iron according to manufacturer's directions. Carefully remove waffle from iron. Serve warm with sugared berries, sweetened whipped cream and syrup drizzle, if desired.

NOTE: Leftover waffles can be frozen; thaw in toaster on low heat or heat in microwave 10 to 15 seconds at MEDIUM (50%).

CRISP PASTRY WAFFLES

MAKES 4 SERVINGS

½ of a 17.3-ounce package **PEPPERIDGE FARM® Puff Pastry Sheets (1 sheet), thawed**

½ **cup hazelnut chocolate spread**

12 **strawberries, sliced**

½ **cup thawed whipped topping**

1. Heat the waffle maker.

2. Unfold the pastry sheet on a work surface. Trim the pastry sheet to fit the waffle maker, if needed. Place the pastry sheet into the waffle maker and close the lid. Cook for 8 minutes or until steaming stops and the waffle is golden brown and crisp.

3. Cut the waffle in quarters. Spread each quarter with 2 tablespoons hazelnut chocolate spread. Top with the strawberries and whipped topping.

ALTERNATE PREPARATION: For waffle sticks, cut the pastry sheet into 6 (about 1½-inches wide) strips. Place into waffle maker and cook as directed above.

FLAVOR VARIATION: You can also try peanut butter topped with sliced banana, honey and chopped pecans or lemon curd topped with marshmallow creme and broiled until the marshmallow creme is lightly browned.

Main Dishes, Sides & Sandwiches

Snacks & Bites

ACKNOWLEDGMENTS

The publisher would like to thank the following companies and organizations listed below for the use of their recipes and photographs in this publication.

Bob Evans®

California Dried Plum Board

Campbell Soup Company

Cream of Wheat®, A Division of B&G Foods North America, Inc.

Florida Department of Citrus

The Hershey Company

Nestlé USA

METRIC CONVERSION CHART

VOLUME MEASUREMENTS (dry)

$^1/_8$ teaspoon = 0.5 mL
$^1/_4$ teaspoon = 1 mL
$^1/_2$ teaspoon = 2 mL
$^3/_4$ teaspoon = 4 mL
1 teaspoon = 5 mL
1 tablespoon = 15 mL
2 tablespoons = 30 mL
$^1/_4$ cup = 60 mL
$^1/_3$ cup = 75 mL
$^1/_2$ cup = 125 mL
$^2/_3$ cup = 150 mL
$^3/_4$ cup = 175 mL
1 cup = 250 mL
2 cups = 1 pint = 500 mL
3 cups = 750 mL
4 cups = 1 quart = 1 L

VOLUME MEASUREMENTS (fluid)

1 fluid ounce (2 tablespoons) = 30 mL
4 fluid ounces ($^1/_2$ cup) = 125 mL
8 fluid ounces (1 cup) = 250 mL
12 fluid ounces (1$^1/_2$ cups) = 375 mL
16 fluid ounces (2 cups) = 500 mL

WEIGHTS (mass)

$^1/_2$ ounce = 15 g
1 ounce = 30 g
3 ounces = 90 g
4 ounces = 120 g
8 ounces = 225 g
10 ounces = 285 g
12 ounces = 360 g
16 ounces = 1 pound = 450 g

DIMENSIONS

$^1/_{16}$ inch = 2 mm
$^1/_8$ inch = 3 mm
$^1/_4$ inch = 6 mm
$^1/_2$ inch = 1.5 cm
$^3/_4$ inch = 2 cm
1 inch = 2.5 cm

OVEN TEMPERATURES

250°F = 120°C
275°F = 140°C
300°F = 150°C
325°F = 160°C
350°F = 180°C
375°F = 190°C
400°F = 200°C
425°F = 220°C
450°F = 230°C

BAKING PAN SIZES

Utensil	Size in Inches/Quarts	Metric Volume	Size in Centimeters
Baking or	8×8×2	2 L	20×20×5
Cake Pan	9×9×2	2.5 L	23×23×5
(square or	12×8×2	3 L	30×20×5
rectangular)	13×9×2	3.5 L	33×23×5
Loaf Pan	8×4×3	1.5 L	20×10×7
	9×5×3	2 L	23×13×7
Round Layer	8×1½	1.2 L	20×4
Cake Pan	9×1½	1.5 L	23×4
Pie Plate	8×1¼	750 mL	20×3
	9×1¼	1 L	23×3
Baking Dish	1 quart	1 L	—
or Casserole	1½ quart	1.5 L	—
	2 quart	2 L	—